REEDS OF BRASS

REEDS OF BRASS

Poems by **Peter Lawlor**
Cover and Drawings by **Margaret Lawlor Bartlett**

2007
FULL MOON PRESS
O
Whidbey Island, Washington.

Other poetry by Peter Lawlor
Nostalgie and Journies 1978
Windsocks and Lyrica 1994
Casting Off 2001

ISBN: 978-0-9644104-2-8
Library of Congress Control Number: 2007900140
Copyright 2007 by Peter Lawlor
Library of Congress Cataloging-in-Publication Data
Published by Full Moon Press
Clinton Washington

Printed by Morris Publishing
3212 East Hwy 30
Kearney Nebraska 68847.

I have a feeling that my boat
has struck, down there in the depths,
against a great thing. And nothing
happens! Nothing.....Silence.....Waves.
　　　　Nothing happens?　Or has everything happened
and are we standing now, quietly, in the new life?.

Juan Ramon Jimenez

Contents

THE CAVALCADE

3. Comrade Stuff
4. Chair of Office
5. The Caregiver
6. The Aquarius
7. The Camelhair Coat
8. Casting the Ashes
9. Along with Hafiz
11. Ships that Pass
12. Odd Things that Follow Great Moments
14. Hebridean Image
15. Tiger
16. Conclave Recalled
17. Poets do Your Gardening
18. Hell's Angels
19. Early Man
20. Sailing Large
21. We're not Getting Blest
22. Declaration
23. Disposal Instructions
24. Not to Bother
25. To the Least Of
26. The Archivist
27. Revolt in the Garden
28. Ski Resort
29. New Outlook
30. Leaving is an Excuse to Come Back
31. Giving It Away
32. Places in the Mind
34. The Old Order Goeth

THE MUSIC

39. Song of the Recorder and Harmonica Players
40. The Bright Light of Angels Is Always
41. Odd Weather
42. Responsibility
43. Adding It All Up
44. Roistering Days
45. Tusitala
46. Leaving Doors Open
47. The Gael
48. Shellback
49. Sea Borne
50. Their Language
51. Long Flight
52. Gourmet
53. Sunday Tea Party
54. You Don't Have To Be Brilliant
55. Motive Gracefully Concealed
56. Everyone
57. Her Body
58. Road Less Taken
59. Winding Back
60. Third Place Books
61. A Laddie and a Lassie / Bonnie Jean
62. Four Score and More

COMRADE STUFF

If it would allow me I would like
To call the computer my friend, my ally.
I know it is asking a lot to have this sophisticate
Sit there and be kind of folksy and let
Me ramble on pulling my images out of
Flotsam on the beach and tea leaves.

Mind you, I approach the intelligent face
Of my computer with the trepidation of
A schoolboy's first day in a class on logic.
I murmur, "Please be easy on me. Could
We work together on this. I am such a dummy."
I must say it is patient with me

Just as long as I don't go prodding it
In sensitive areas and be aware it has its feelings.
I rather like the way we say hullo as we start the day.
If it had a tail it would wag as I pat the opening key.
We get into discussions right away, no need
To waste time in the bathroom primping up.

Mutual respect is the essence of our relationship.
It knows I am creative; I know its wealth of knowledge.
My face meets its face as personally as the wedded.
We share human traits in being complicated
It can be bitchy and I can be testy. Nobody's perfect.
We are getting to know each other.

Seattle
Washington
Sept. 2006

CHAIR OF OFFICE

I can't remember a specific time
when I was handed authority
to conduct this life of mine.
My parents, assured as the straight backed
oaken chairs around the dining table,
never handed over keys. I was smacked
as a small boy and Mum brushed
my hair on Sundays when I went to Mass
and was given money for the plate,
which didn't credit me for much.
I needed establish my own estate.

So I left to make my own investiture;
signed on ship and went away to sea.
There was money in it but a dicey future.
So invested what I made in wife and we
brought up children, cats and dogs,
which takes a measure of command.
My Dad said later sadly, "I never knew you son."
It wasn't too late. He shook my hand.
He was allowing something I had won.
And now I sit in the straight backed oaken chair
where, regardless of the keys,
there's much authority invested there .

At "Tusitala"
Whidbey Island
October 2002

THE CAREGIVER

When I was small we had a special aunt
always coming in the door, sometimes knocking.
When war was declared we all sat down and changed
because things were happening beyond us.
Yet things couldn't happen without her.
Nor had anything scraped by without her stamp.
The baby sister who appeared when we thought
no more would come, came with her announcement.
She wore aprons for times like that. I helped her folding sheets.
We picked gooseberries in grandmother's place.
Our aunt lived there and cared for her as well.
Only one man in her life - he went away to war -
wrote her a letter. She threw his ring into a lake.
She taught school and told us stories about America
and the world we were growing into.
She told us more than Mum or Dad had dared.
Everything was changing. We tried to understand.
One day hanging clothes on the line she fell.
Never got out of bed again. It was her spine.
Then Mum and she spent hours and hours on the phone.

Wellington
New Zealand.

THE AQUARIUS

What ferry are you on
my woman, my wedded vow?
Do I see Aquarius
painted on the prow?
Where is she headed for?
Does your captain say?
Your light glows intermittently
in the night sky.

What do you gaze upon
my bed-mate, my golden one?
Do you navigate by the stars?
Does the mate plot the sun
to get a bearing on your course?
How many fathoms do you sound?
After berthing does
the ferry turn around?

Who walks the deck with you,
my tiger, my old love,
a sailor, one of the crew?
Do you talk of the sea
or the land that you knew?
As your ship draws near
the elemental shore
have you excitement, or fear?.

Under what flag does she sail
my old lady, my willful one?
Do you disembark
into clouds on that run?
Do they unship the gangway
so you can step ashore?
This is all speculation.
I won't ask any more.

Cascade Beach
Whidbey Island
July 2001

THE CAMELHAIR COAT

It was a windy day in Wellington
at a corner by Lambton Quay.
We were introduced, I don't recall words
but your camelhair coat brings it back;
the way that you stood, your eyes were big.
I remember those street meetings.
I waited watching you come,
collar up and the stepping.
You walked magnificently.
Shoes were important.
Details plotted our lives..
Were your ways and your style there in that coat?
It was more than just shelter from wind.

New Zealand
Val's Anniversary
18th July 2004

CASTING THE ASHES
(fulfilling my wife's request to scatter her ashes upon a Scottish lake)

In a crescent shape it hovered
A white cloud above Loch Maree
Her spirit found a place once traveled
To, where it was wont to be.
I read our daughter's prayer and a song
As the spirit settled down
To the golden rocks where the long
Glen rose from the Scottish depths
To the summit of Slioch above -
A completion of the task she wished,
It was a tough demand of love.

She wasn't one to take all for granted
And might have been surprised I carried it out.
She was stubborn, in some ways slanted,
Denied Irish, said she was a Scot.
Well there she is, I took her back.
I gave her benefit of the doubt.

Scottish Highlands
July 2006

ALONG WITH HAFIZ

The poet can laugh with God
Not feeling guilty about having to say
Morning prayers with serious face
And suffer with sores like Job.
The poet can say anything he pleases
Especially to God ; give him a bit of hell
And expect a lot back -
Peppered with wit.
And both roll back in their chairs
Laughing their heads off.

The laughter of God has a great range
Scaling octaves which the poet can match
Being vocally unfettered.
The poet and God go hand in hand
Out on the town
Visiting the dingiest dives.
Neither is a stuffed shirt
So they join in the fun un-noticed.

That is the beauty of being a poet
Having fun, on a par with God
And not feeling favored.
Bystanders can't believe this,
Seeing the inequality
Of this companionship.
Some throw stones.
The poet shrugs this off
Having the armor of being
Totally absorbed in the love
Of people and towns where bells ring
For prayers and laughter.

God and the poet love the lovers;
The not so wimpy saints
Like Augustine, Therese, and
Whitman who wasn't a saint,
But each had the guts
And the irreverence which
Goes along with reverence.
They had a knack of
Getting along with God.

Whidbey Island
June 2006

SHIPS THAT PASS

And so we meet , then we are gone.
From ship to ship across the water
we hail and wave and sing our song.
The flags are all run up, our mooring ropes
seem to tie us all together.
We walk and talk along the decks
into the night, then morning comes.
Gangways are raised
On the dock a band plays.
Anchors are weighed.
We cast off, and all our farewells
are dashed in the wake
like floating flowers.
On the horizon a distant port.
We count the days and miles
before next landfall and when
we might meet again.
But each ship plots a different course.
That's the way it has always been.

Langley
Whidbey Island   WA
November 2005

ODD THINGS THAT FOLLOW GREAT MOMENTS

The picture of Tolstoy in his eighties chopping wood
inspires me, particularly the freedom of
the white peasant blouse he wears;
the practicality of the garment allowing
free swing of the axe which tells me
he is not posing but means business.

When such realism is pictured
I like to take it on to the next stage,
for instance Tolstoy taking a bath afterwards,
a great beard settling on to the soapy surface.
But no, it would be in a tub outside
under an apple tree – a skim of ice
on the surface, the blouse hung on a branch.

It is not easy for me to picture
the bathroom scene of Queen Victoria after
a hard day of posing for massive bronze sculptures.
On the other hand quite easy to visualize
Marie Antoinette at her toilette, roses floating
in a bath shaped like a shell,
a pearl or two embedded in the rim.

With such dull routine stuff going on in my life
I like to lay the equivalent on the great,
figuring how they handled socks for the laundry.
And did Teddy Roosevelt while taking off his belt
and riding breeches heave a sigh and start
issuing exhortations for empire expansions.

Not stretching my imagination there is J.P.Morgan
removing his frock coat at home after
the limousine has deposited him in his sun court,
and in waist coat with gold fob struggles
between a whiskey and stock market reports.

The other thing would be, in the event
I should ever write an immortal line,
would anyone be interested
to find out that I had laid down my pen
and went out into the garden to hack
at the hedge with a machete.

Whidbey Island Cottage
September 2006

HEBRIDEAN IMAGE

The image of a fishwife comes to mind.
I can't get rid of it. She comes out of my
Background of the sea. She's fierce
And strong, sitting with tartan apron
All messy, and she sings in a high pitch
Angrily, about her husband out at sea.

He is no good; a dreamer seaborne, playing
A love song to a water sprite, when he
Should be netting the shoals of herring.
His fishwife knows that part of him
So well and once loved allowing it.
Now she kicks the fish bucket to even up.

I am always looking at wonderful women
Thinking they might be of the sea,
Faces hidden by blowing hair that parts
A fragmentary moment to reveal
The one you long for above all others,
That Ianthe whose name is written in the sand.

They are staunch these women of the Hebrides
With strong ankles, well formed from striding
In the seaweed and pulling the tarred boats ashore.
The fisherman should bear in mind that though
They might yell and dress him down they make,
With their strong bodies, the finest wives.

Portree
Isle of Skye
August 2003

TIGER

I dreamt about an orange cat.
It was large. "Take your arm off,"
a voice said. I didn't care.
I wanted it to be my friend,
grow larger yet and maybe dangerous.
It curled around the corner by the door.
I thought to stir it with my foot.
Then it might not like my shoe.
It demanded respect, its eyes
so sleepy full of old fire and great
looked up a moment, the lids
closed languidly leaving me
in need. The sun shone on
its markings, yellow in the gold
and black, as embers in a flame.
I think the black smoldered
in the orange, making the cat
more tiger-like. That was where
the thought of ownership began
taking hold of me obsessively.
I wanted the cat more and more.
I wanted fear to be in my life –
around the house. When it grew
in the years to come it might attack
and I would struggle ineffectually
and in a fateful moment resign.
Then it would walk away and
leave me, with that casual air
that attracted me so.
Yes, I'd take the chance.

Seaman's Cottage
Cascade Beach
April 2006

CONCLAVE RECALLED

Once we gathered as a group of fishermen.
We met in the high places where rivers were
and lakes lay like cats in the laps of mountains.
We lit a fire and told our stories laughing
long into the listening night air for we
were ever there and would never leave.
Fortunate few we were, thrown together
like leaves that gather in autumn days.
In the morning with the sun we walked,
confident as the first creatures on earth,
sharing with ancient fish the glowing streams.
So much was given to us we did not hear the bell.
Now we haven't met in years and may not again.
Nonetheless the stream is there, and the lake
is quiet now where we never left.

In the West
May 12th 2006

EARLY MAN

He has to tell you about the bones
and shells glued into the desert face
where the sea washed a million years ago.
It's pretty dry stuff to listen to
in a coffee shop at morning break.
But this guy has to be seventy
going on a thousand,
so you allow the dialogue.
His eyes hold you.
You suspect they are blue,
yet they may be stone .
His face is not wrinkled,
time pacing the years
not having to leave notation.
There is a look that doesn't
belong to him any more,
and a voice from down the years.
It is past coffee time
and some have left.
Our busy world doesn't cope
easily with the dust of paleontology.
Today's paper lies there
with the weather forecast
and what they are saying in important cities,
stuff that has no bearing on his story.
He is lost in his artifacts.
They are assembled, patiently tagged
And dry, with a million years.

The Bakery
Langley
Whidbey Island
April 2006

SAILING LARGE

He wrote a card to me to say
he'd signed on to go back to sea
on a sailing ship no less, and to confess
he'd been down in the dumps, all grey.

There's a depression that seamen get
when they're stranded back on land.
It's like beached whales
that thrash in the sand
inscribing their epitaph.

A big man, he'll be strong on the yard,
hanging there furling sails,
a black bat in the sky,
tarred feet on the ratlines
and the white salt roiling far below.

We worked on a freighter in the Vietnam war
in the sixties and I felt the same as he,
all bragged up and swaggering
I threw in my able seaman card -
the voyage was less than a year,
while he took it up for life; all that strife
fighting up - bosun, mate, master.

I want to reply; "What's your grief Chief?
You're away like a sheet in the wind.
I'm stuck on the land, gardening in the sand
in my cottage by the sea."

Well that's why he's there and I'm here.
We have to come back and complain.
Like Masefield the poet we must go back
to the sea again, lonely with the sky
with our ills in our gills, spitting salt
into old rope worn hands.

Burning Wood Poetry Event
Greenbank
Whidbey Island Washington
April 2005

WE'RE NOT GETTING BLEST

Looking out from our pressurized portholes
Clouds appear- ceremonial lumps of heaven.
Saints sit in them on silver chairs.
There's a feeling that if you knelt on one
Of their summits you might get a blessing.
Planes are newcomers violating clouds' serenity.
Clouds held sway long before we ventured.
As we descend slicing with vulgar wings,
We tear at their immortal bodies.
No wonder that clouds toss us around,
Taunting and snatching like cats with a rat.
We're lucky to get out alive.

Above Newark
July 2006

DECLARATION

What to declare at the border?
I have to hide stuff or
I'll never make it. They don't suspect,
but really I'm carrying baggage
that wouldn't make it at a tribunal.

If they knew the killing I've done
with the pointed word - the look-
that I've lied and perjured for baubles,
that I'm on the run from debtors
who would claim what remains of soul,
I'd be detained for interrogation.

They won't find a weapon
amongst the underhand betrayals
all ditched long ago.
My bag of shirts, sox and trinkets
is a cover up, the layer of everyman.
I sail through at the checkpoint.

Another guy out there is getting
worked over and it's only because
he's tattooed and beer bellied -
trunk lid open, an old jalopy -
not a hope. They'll find something.

My declaration is bland and
I'm such a clean looking liar.
A stamped passport is my absolution.
I exit this border confessional
murmuring an act of contrition.
Later I sit at a side-walk café,
contraband tucked away in the bag at my feet.

German/Polish Border
August 2003

DISPOSAL INSTRUCTIONS

A shipmate sent me burial procedure at sea.
I looked at it carefully. It pertains to me.
I told him I wished to be cradled in canvas
Sewn up with a cannon ball at my feet,
With a splash to enter my future in the deep.

It was a daunty request that required the bearers
To know nautical details. They would be sharers
Of responsibility. The sail maker's thread
Must go through my chin in the canvas bag
To hold my head up so the rest doesn't sag.

There's cotton to be stuffed in the nose and mouth,
A sling under my jaw so it doesn't jut south,
Arms folded across chest like Nelson or Napoleon.
I would be slid from the scuppers of a worthy vessel,
Piped from the poop deck with all at attention.

I would like to select a captain who was jovial.
No tears at the taffrail, no bowed head at the burial.
He would crack a joke and innuendo at the requiem.
I'd want a bosun who knew leeward from windward
So I wouldn't catch a wave and come back again.

Now here's the prayers I would like to have said:
"Ship me out fast. Sling me from my bed.
Stow round shot at feet to prop me up straight.
Let me face the fast fishies on an equal footing.
No resting in peace at my Watergate!"

For Captain Ray Conrady (Merchant Marine)
San Francisco
California
June 1st 2006

NOT TO BOTHER

I am not dismayed when I complete
My little death, my normal nightly sleep.
I am not aware of being taken from the scene
Of having obligations, things that mean
Having to balance bank statements and bills,
Fix leaking roof, find pills for aging ills.
So if I keep on sleeping for years and years
And stars come out and go and no more tears,
Someone else has to tidy up and mend the gate-
Routine stuff that kept me in a state
Of putting things off dodging responsibility
Giving my Celtic shoulder shrug of futility.
So meanwhile, this other, this interim,
This little bit of dying, awakening bright,
Rehearsal for the long slow dying of the light
Does not dismay; both sleeps are gentle places
To come in and out of easy dreaming spaces.

The Planet
No fixed time and place

TO THE LEAST OF

Birds skitter,
loose as scraps
of paper below
the shaking stark
lilac branches.
Cold rain
comes again.
An old man
sits inside
the seeing window
looking out
rather absently.
He puts on a coat.
It's a dozen steps
and a cupful of seed
from the door
to the bird feeder.
That's not a bad
bit of charity

Cascade Beach
Whidbey Island
November 2005

THE ARCHIVIST

He has a peculiar joy of wrestling
garments out of closets and assembling
the complete person and the period,
knowing families revel in disclosing
their bit of bastardry - if it's noble.
They want to know which uncle kept
a bodkin in his watch fob pocket
to settle pesky arguments and
which distant cousin was deported
just for snaring a rabbit for lunch.
He has a storage mind for detail.
Well told it comes to life.
The old motor cars huff and puff
and husbands drive away on assignations.
Polite people with hats doff
and bow so grandly insincerely.
A grandma all corseted and quietly wicked
is documentary best seller stuff.
He delights in digging out data -
frisky foibles in the blood lines.
Then families sit around a table deliciously
digesting their fare of blemished ancestry.

Novato
2005/2006

REVOLT IN THE GARDEN

Silently so much is happening.
While there are armies
Who have to bivouac at night.
These have no such respite.
Under cover of black soil
An arterial vein-work
Of lacy fingers probe
The darkness for the force
That will send green spears
Lancing the surface -
Cohorts gleaming,
Into the marching world.
There, wind with its urgent
Voice beckons those with banners
To join in the parade.
Above, the spring boughs
Laden white for the occasion
Flag on the newcomers.
The music – "Marche Militaire"
And creatures that dare to leap
Entreat underlings to get started.
A lily unwraps its lazy shawl.
And primroses with their wondering eyes
Are astounded at the world around.
A lawn spreads out its official robe
Hung with medals of ceremony.
In the ferns, bracken that stood
Low in the winter air, a bed
To nurture the unfolding-
That agreement of silence
While tubers were birthing
Is now broken, and the wild
Plum trees who obey
No laws whatsoever toss
Their pink manifesto into the wind
Shouting revolution, and nothing
Can be still any more this summer.

At the Cottage
Clinton Washington
May 2006

SKI RESORT

Do you remember kicking steps in the snow Mollie?
I recall the fur collar that covered your throat.
Yes, my daring discovery of the warmth of your lips.
I was bold, young, you were older than I.
I couldn't believe what I'd done. Did you know
That kiss awakened and destroyed?
It squandered the purse of my heart.
So I signed on a ship to try to get even
And sail away from the hurt.
Did you suffer at all? I don't think you did.
The sea modified the pain that I felt.
But your touch and the taste of your lips
Returned over and over again.
I wonder if you knew what you'd done Mollie
With steps in the snow and the fur at your throat
The skill you knew well, my boldness, my first,
Making all later loves a replay.

Chateau Tongariro
New Zealand
1940   (re-written 2006)

NEW OUTLOOK

Having bought the place
and done the fix ups
I came upon myself
in the woody parlor,
there with teapot
befriending the sea.
A lot had happened -
(a filing drawer full of it.)
There were closures
in which the heart
is seldom consulted.
A new home is sought
and old one waved goodbye.
Uprootings are cold.
They are like ships
leaving port; no one
standing at the stern
after the lines are stowed.
Some furniture is shipped
following like dogs
from the last house.
I was pleased to notice
curtains were new,
and though the exchanged
windows and doors
kept surprising me,
mirrors kept their old familiarity.
I felt at home with things.
Is that what one calls
"Casting off?"
The sea has definitely
something to do with it.

Seaman's Cottage
Whidbey Island
February 2005

LEAVING IS AN EXCUSE TO COME BACK

The lady has to make a journey and all
the ordinary things will wait in their place
while she is gone. The green buds will hold out.
It is too cold to show, but there are shoots
under black soil which will go down for water.
Trees apologize, so bare they cannot halt the wind.
Their leaves will later make a barricade.
Dogs will be there waiting all their lives.
Tides which come and go year long
are expected to make a difference at the shore.
Her house, which stays the same, is the mountain
to which one returns after the trek and
where it is necessary to kneel and light the fire.

Cascade Beach
Whidbey Island
February 2006

GIVING IT AWAY

Two old geezers meet in a bookshop.
Each one knows he hasn't yet found life's clue.
So they begin laughing about it knowing
the fun's in the gambit, the posing,
the blather, the bon mot that's not true,
showing you can't pose right
if you don't know you're shamming,
you have to keep feigning a fight.
They know it's boring to have to keep listening
to someone great in his boots blustering.
So they walk around the bookshelves
affecting interest in the odd tome or two;
no bookish remarks, just tongue lashing each other-
that joyous stuff street dogs do.

The bookshop is a stage set for a play with
two old dogs who don't give the show away
in barking out a platitude with an uppity attitude.
They know the truth is what nonsense can say.

Golden Otter Bookshop
Langley, WA.
March 2005

PLACES IN THE MIND

It's those snippets of what we did that fascinate,
That keep the mind tumbling over its toes with "Was it real?"
The elderberries seething in the bucket in Devon;
The brigadier put me up to it. He said,
"They grow in the hedgerows. Everyone makes wine."
We rented his mansion for a year or so.
His dog came with the deal, a Jack Russell.
"Does she bite?" I asked his wife. "Only if she doesn't like you."
Dogs were always in our lives after that - all ladies.
It was houses of our lives that set the scene:
The little one in Sausalito on a side street
Up from the theatre and the beach. We had cats then.
One of them was Laurence named after a friend.
They both had ginger hair. Laurence cat had
The softest purr - like an engine left running.
It was bits of events that marked the memory.
It wasn't the bigger things like a broken leg
At Sun Valley that almost ended my ski teaching career
Or the avalanche. It was snippets like the pink dirndls our
Little girls wore after the snows left in the spring.
A Swiss made them. She made fondue too.
In the summer Val rode a horse named Mirabel. I fished.
Four winters there and then we never went back.
Went back to the one in Mill Valley California, where
Val hung fuchsias from the porch, dark purple and pink,
Below the redwoods. The ghosts had fled.
They only stay a while when you leave a house.
New people change things, that's why. It's sad.
Change interferes with memories. There were three dogs
We had in Santa Fe, buried on a mound behind the house,
Sarah, the greatest, was wild, part wolf; swam the
Rio Grande in full flood, bank to bank. Val
Planted native trees out front - not easy in the desert.
I can't expect new owners to reverence the mound.
Dogs run in the mind for always, and things
Like garden gates you painted are done over –
wind vane taken down and bushes grown over dog's graves.

Things don't hang around for your return
even if the doorbell sounds the same.
It's just good to tumble the snippets around.

At the Cottage
Whidbey Island
June 2006

THE OLD ORDER GOETH

When you see the notice it hits you with a thump:
Your favorite coffee house is closing down.
It isn't fair. Where will Willard go, and Herb
The clock maker; he'll be nonplussed.
And all those faces buried in the daily news,
Yes, too, the poet who wrote at these tables,
They will all have to find another room.
You know the whole ménage is being served notice.
Boswell will have to lead his Johnson through another door.

All the furor and talk that could have filled
A hundred plays will be stopping now.
Able seaman Roy (retired) won't be nibbling on his scone.
You're desolate that his blather will be silenced – gone.
They'll switch the table cloths from beneath the saucers.
Marilyn's ladies' circle will dissolve as nebulously
As the sugar in their loquacious coffee cups.

You know that from the ashes a new place doesn't rise
Right away, and regulars don't get up en mass
To find a quick replacement, No they filter
Testing other haunts where chairs and tables must allow
Elbows, the outdoor light must slide across the shoulder.
You must have walls not too remote so folks can bump
Into each other and apologize. You know the kind of place.

You worry the replacement coffee shop won't have the smell.
There's concern that some voices will not be heard again,
That folks will give up and latte-up at home.
Then word gets around that dear bone man Dale was spotted
In a bookshop-cum-coffee house with dog or woman,
Either one, or both. You're desperate but you know
The ranks are forming. Do not fear - Nil Desperandum.

Langley
Whidbey Island
Sept 25th 2006

FOR DEBORAH

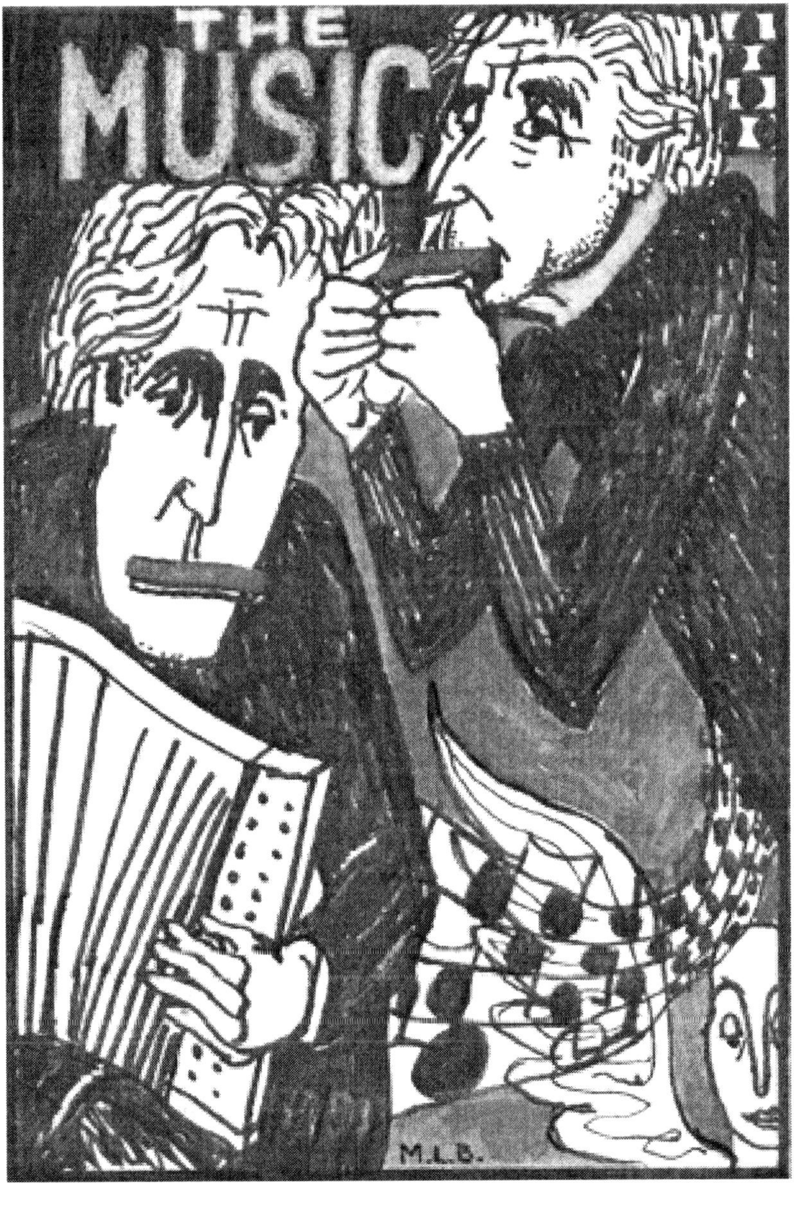
THE
MUSIC
M.L.B.

SONG OF THE RECORDER AND HARMONICA PLAYERS

You were growing up
and slender even then.
I too growing
sparse in frame,
and it was when
our music came.

Fortunate we were
hungry for the song.
We sat on the porch
in the morning sun.
We needed a leader
then he came along.

Music was a wanderer
in rags and hungry too.
He came down the street,
it was lucky that you
asked him in to sit.
Then we sang his song.

And we still hunger
for his wayward ditty;
Greensleeves, the Ash Grove
and Dublin's Fair City.
That wandering minstrel
we hold him fast,
you in the cherry wood,
I in reeds of brass.

Novato
California
Deborah's Birthday
May 1999

THE BRIGHT LIGHT OF ANGELS IS ALWAYS

And too, the bright voice of angels is always.
Angels are aware of this and only speak
words of their own and we must listen.
There is an impatience about them;
visitations are bestowed, bright and rare.

Daughters are angels flashing across
the sky, dropping into our lives for a time.
We cannot keep them, they have a mission.
Such angels have to be allowed room.
They have an immense amount of work
that has to be executed gracefully, deftly,
because their touch is of a wingtip.
Strange that it leaves such a mark.

Poem of Two Hemispheres
8th Jan 2006.

ODD WEATHER

It's been a good day with things done.
As I say, "That's good" my breath
comes back with: "Deb's dead."
Is my voice saying that?
They are the strangest words.
I have never heard them before.
Therefore they don't belong.
I am discrediting them right now.

Then a sickening thought sinks in;
And it says coldly, "Yes."
The good day is now hollow
The guts have gone out of it.
I hang on to doubting.
Why is it after good things are done,
and it should be warming,
that the cold questions come?

I wash the dishes and
find myself talking to her.
"What did you think, Deb,
when you saw all of your life
and it became so brilliant?"
My questions are rhetorical
but they help fill in the holes.

Poetry helps. There was a poem
I wrote for Deb about
a garden chair in Mill Valley.
She was always sitting there.
I look at the wicker chair
by the fire in my living room.
It gives me a kind of comfort
So I'll take it out in the garden
tomorrow if this weather picks up.

Whidbey Island
January 2006.

RESPONSIBILITY

Why should I moan because you
no longer watch the eagle with me?
Your soul may be that great bird.
Should I be distraught because you
no longer cast the fly line by my river?

You caught two splendid trout one day.
Perhaps that was enough, you kept one.
The other may be finning its rainbow
flanks in the stream where we stood.
Is it you?

And if I complain of the rain
so constant in the north I must recall
with what religious fervor
you welcomed it.

You would run in the rain rejoicing.
You may be in the cloud unleashing
sheets of rain. It's so green here.
Are you responsible?

For Deborah
Cascade Beach
Whidbey Island
May 2006

ADDING IT ALL UP

Good men at my age don't fret passing of hours.
In their quiet rooms they hear rhapsodies and allow
waiting days to be filled free and easy, and music
to dance lightly in dusty corners.

Years back there might have been
some dismay because a day
slipped by like a lean wind, thin
as paper, blank, with no accounting.

It's all that tabulating, enumerating things
eating into time allowed that bothers.
Whereas a good stack of years piled
on a desk in the memoirs room
add up to a grand number.
Music gathers there - old opera scores,
love lyrics, waist coated tenors, divas
on stages littered with flowers.

No wonder old men don't fret passing of hours
with such notes, such performances.

Seattle
September 2003

ROISTERING DAYS

I was a loose lad on a merchant ship
It was years ago – forty-two,
A good crew, kippers for breakfast;
To Glasgow up the river Clyde.
Now the years jump, they do that
Giving snippets, just bits in the mind –
Recall dance halls in the blackout,
The leaving and a kiss on the dock.
You have to keep a favorite land;
It isn't the place you live now,
It's where you did what you did before
So you go there to break routine
And dreaming brings back the scene.

I'm looking down on the river Clyde,
The old nautical eye from a plane.
It's distracting with all this folderol
About seat belts. They don't understand.

Glasgow
Scotland
July 2006

TUSITALA

The sea comes to me
out of its old birthplace
telling me of its achievements -
how it carried ships,
sometimes taking them -
boasting about its storms.
I would like it to be
not so egotistical.
The sea speaks -
does not listen.
All I can do is
hear out its voice
and take heed
without taking offense,
then wait for my moment.

I would like to have my say,
pick up a shell and yell.
I have stories too.
I have named my house,
on this trembling shore,
"Tusitala"- the teller of tales.
Stevenson took on that name
in the islands of Samoa
as he wrote of the sea.

Cascade Beach
Whidbey Island
July 2002

LEAVING DOORS OPEN

I join the old sailor by his door
and we talk the sort of things -
words rattling in hollow beer cans,
not much of account, only old ramblings.
But our eyes convey a lot so it need
not be clever, contrived, or fashionable.
All that's needed is to be here having
the door open all day, all night.
No one can rob us, all valuables
are there for the taking, that way
we can talk and not be afraid.

We have values that have little
to do with the economy
but varied as a deck cargo.
Our minds deal with a jumble
of flags and latitudes,
Alaska and Wild Bill,
Black guys we'd worked with,
The stakes in a card game,
Name of a street somewhere –
Mutual stuff we recall
Songs we had forgotten -
Songs seamen slinging in hammocks
Sang on decks – leaving doors open.

It's a kind of invitation.
Who knows, maybe a poet like Coleridge
might happen to drop in, holding us with
his Mariner of skinny hand and glittering eye.

Ivan's Place
Saratoga passage
Puget Sound
August 2003

THE GAEL

Beyond the bar a trio sang the Celtic songs.
He knew the words, and drinking hard joined in.
It might have bothered them. I liked his ways;
Being a noisy singer myself we had a bond.
"No one knows the Gaelic words," he said,
"Though they might know the tune." That's sad.
We asked them play "Shoals of Herring"
Which the trio didn't know So we sang
"Fiddlers Green" noisily, which they let us do.
A big Scot he looked into my eyes and his were bright.

They hold their drinks with joy, I thought, these Celts.
And listeners might shy away politely. What a loss.
No nuisance me. When you sing together
Nothing matters. The thing was, we were traveling on.
"We will not meet again," he said.
I caught the long look I've seen in seamen's eyes
When we signed off a voyage parting on the dock.
There was a reluctant sadness in it.
So in my mind I sang the last line of the song:
"And I'll see you someday in Fiddlers Green."

Leaving Scotland
July 2006

SHELLBACK

All you need is a glimpse of the sea through curtains.
Once it was the whole horizon lavish
with pink castles changing into dragons-
the selfish joy of loneliness in the sea lanes
and the boy-man you hankered to be.

You signed on for foreign ports
and the crew told you the best hangouts.
Your father wrote a letter with a dozen stamps.
You were the bold one with the gold tooth.
Your family fancied you under many flags.

A couple of times you changed nationalities.
After the storms you built a picket fence.
Boundaries are good after all that freedom.
With a red sky – sailor's warning, and
barking of dogs, the air is somehow your own.

You stand at the gate beyond the curtains.
You fancy yourself a bit.
Very small children stare at you scared
 hiding behind mother's skirts peeking.
That is not a bad acclaim;
They imagine you as their Captain Hook.

Cascade Beach
February 2006

SEA BORNE

Out along the sea before my house
a log came floating by upon the tide.
From what quiet forest had it come?
What earth message went through its roots?
It seemed to have a built-in plan of voyage.
That craft didn't want to beach itself.
It rolled lazily as a swell came by
independent and not suggesting me aboard.
And I've been on a few odd craft;
shipped out, not knowing destination
or caring. We weren't told port in wartime.
Now I am uprooted from earth too
and I felt a kinship with that seaward log -
no fixed port - that's like the Polynesians -
let birds tell you where there's land.

A seagull boarded and stood a watch
upon my log and they floated far along
until the gull, its pilot, indicated
when shore and tide were right for landing.
Then beached at high tide mark, along with others
bearing marks of passage, just as I have,
the log has joined the sand to spend a season
with me, until a storm shifts our berth.
Then up and on we go seaward once again.

Cascade Beach
Whidbey Island
February 2003

THEIR LANGUAGE

Dogs in the morning dusk of sleep share
their radiant body-blankets upon my bed.
They tell me softly of a whole week
of sleep they had last night, their soft eyes
dancing with a kind of delight in telling.
What sort of language is this they use?
It isn't French, Romanian or Latin.
It's just dog, It isn't anything else.
It keeps on being said and I'm learning
there is no alphabet within the mind.
Something is said that can't be read;
no design or page to make a statement
with crafty woven phrase. It's getting rid
of words and just using a telling position.
There's a stance that conveys thoughts like:
"I'll give you a whole day of loving.
There's food for both, enough for all."

Now as I write for them I must discard the words.
They don't need them
They know what I have written.

Whidbey Island
October 3rd 2002

LONG FLIGHT

He shot the bird who stood along the beach.
Stealthily, no click of cartridge into breach.
I heard the shots, the echo quickly died
Like a departing soul winging wide.
It was a heron- a useless shot, it fell
A limp rag rolling in the swell.
The hidden marksman left it lying on the sand.
Well, now my mornings have no bird to stand
Long legged, intent, slim, silver grey,
Patient as a priest invoking day.
It's dead, and somehow better off than we –
That one with gun, coldly unaware that he
Lives on not loving himself, not knowing blame
And I to never see that long slow flight again.

Cascade View Beach
Whidbey Island
July 2006

GOURMET

What has been created in my kitchen today
is in my mind a masterpiece, unique, unrecorded,
the likes of which will not be seen again.
There it is, don't laugh, a pot of chili,
Chili con carne, yes indeed mi Corazon.
And you could say the Soul went into it too.

Before walking away let us consider ingredients.
It is the mystery of the bean, tight fisted relic,
ancestor that takes me by the hand into old pueblos.
It is the bedrock of my dish – the adobe.

I lay out the green chili; it yields to my dissecting
knife, organs revealed, seeds suspended
from the central aorta, living breathing.
Such chili when red could form a ristra.

The Jalapeno says not a word of its power,
a small mighty general with no need for a horse.
Beware, do not rub the eyes
with the hand that has met this master.

Tomato is queen with its ladies in waiting
proceeding from my garden; of mysterious lineage
suspected of links with the nightshade.
I feel honored to be involved in the mystery.

With such a complement how can I hold my cool.
You have to allow my ravings. I am a kitchen lover,
wild rover of the pots, a dash of this and that,
delirious over the perfect omelet, the enchilada,
the chili, the likes of which will not be seen again.

Cottage Kitchen
Whidbey Island
September 2006

SUNDAY TEA PARTY
or how to maintain decorum.
(after Noel Coward)

You don't need much;
just a small affair -
teacups that chink
the straight backed chair.
And it isn't wrong
while sipping tea
to balance a scone
upon the knee
along with tasteful talk
that need not be
noticeably alarming
nor loud of voice.
One can be charming
and feel all right
saving the breath
for a liberal fight
by bringing up weather
to a militant right.

It's a good idea
to toss in the air
tidbits of trivia
at such an affair.

Oh it's nice to be nice
at a Sunday tea party
And it does suffice
to be not too arty.

Be deceptively calm
Take tea, slowly sip,
take time to re-arm.
On shoulder - no chip.
Steady cup on saucer,
straighten back, bite lip.

Whidbey Island
October 2004

YOU DON'T HAVE TO BE TOO BRILLIANT

This fumbling old romantic soul
Picks up a rake or anything to hand
To beat the air. The truth is
I am conducting orchestras,
My baton enticing the player
Who recognizes and shares passion,
Which could be so in the matter of cooking-
Adding the right herb with a flourish, then
Walking away, hands raised with the pride of it.

I suppose it is alright to brandish
These scattered talents and not be awed
In the presence of laureates and the Nobel Prize
I am good at pruning the branches
Of the plum tree to make it
Supplicate the sky, poetically.

Clinton
Washington
November 2005

MOTIVE GRACEFULLY CONCEALED

An eagle drifted by on lazy wings.
Indolent as it appeared, it caused a ripple.
Crows saw it and told friends to form a nuisance
squad and make ungraceful swoops.

Sparrows knew it was too high and didn't skitter
Birdwatchers reported it as number ninety seven
which didn't do it justice. Could have given it
a name, Icarus perhaps, or Cleo.

Drivers in cars couldn't pull off and gawk;
only a glance, wishing better opportunity.
The bird, a mature one worth a look; the image
an Indian when the dance begins.

It circled on a thermal, then mapped the shore,
still casual as a millionaire with more wealth
than needed, but that was only a ploy
and talons dropped from the sky to hook the fish.

The troller in a boat looked on outclassed.
If he'd caught a salmon he didn't have such style.
The eagle, flapping now, not quite as casual
with heavy cargo slung beneath, but so confident.

Cascade Beach
Whidbey Island
March 2006

EVERYONE

I try to tell you not to be dismayed.
Everyone tries to do what's to be done.
Alright, you went to Mexico for Christmas
Then called me, lonely because family
Should be together in their own kind of weather.
I wanted to say "Celebrate." Celebrate lonely.
Celebrate the long trek in difficult shoes –
You went across Asia, carried a pack.
Celebrate the day in Vancouver
When you were born. We rented rooms...
Celebrate the house you built together -
Then he left. You carried on.
Celebrate your children who love you.
Sometimes you thought they didn't.
Celebrate raising them and dogs and cats.
Celebrate old sins and things that don't hurt anymore.

In Mexico you said they came, eight million
To venerate the Virgin of Guadalupe.
You all sang and cried. She consoled.
Some hobbled miles to celebrate,
And they were poor. They were not dismayed.
What an achievement – all those feet...

Seattle
Christmas 2006

HER BODY
(to Talia)

A woman picks up the violin.
She loves it as much as
The mother who has just
Given birth to a child.
She cradles her violin.
It is of her womb.
She lowers her chin
On to its smoothness
Smiling the look
Of the lost-in-love.
Then it is played upon
In the manner of one
Who has abandoned
All earthly touch.

The woman dances
Upon the ceiling
With her violin.
It has wings.
She sails on a pond.
The bow in her hands
Becomes an oar.
She leaps into the air.
The violin is a sail.
It is alight in its voice -
Trembling, magnificent.
Tenderly now the woman
Bends and succors it.
It receives all she has.
The violin is lost
In her body

Island Coffee House
Langley
September 2006.

ROAD LESS TAKEN
(Apologies to Robert Frost)

She says she couldn't find the phone,
then found it on the second call
under the laundry pile which she
thought had been done, but wasn't.
My hopes weren't high I heaved a sigh.
We're all in this together.

Her car keys disappeared
and it was fortunate the third set
only to be used in case of fire,
turned up slightly damp in a strange place.
Her second set was written off as lost.
The fourth, in a lock box under a fender
now forgotten, faded into antiquity.

Life proceeds with these pings
of loss and sweet reunion.
Times and places are jotted
in trusty appointment books
while the cruel clock races
and we can't find the places,
settling for somewhere else instead.

It doesn't matter much because
we've forgotten the names of the ones
we actually set out to meet.
To overcome shortcomings we find
friends similar, and glorious reunions
result with strangers who likewise
made a turn onto the road less taken.

Kirkland
Washington
Ongoing 2006

WINDING BACK

When I think that once we wound the watch
each morning and poured cream from a bottle of milk,
lit taper to the stove from matches, did things
now done for us by science, there's left a hole.
This we fill by buying new technology; pay for it
on line, which seemingly saves time, and still we whine.
We can't go backwards, buttons are here to push.
We wouldn't want to crank the car again and break a wrist.
And just because we ride a bike in protest of emissions
we won't give up our motherly womb, the car.
I fear the cell phone is here and will shape the ear
and make our talking into public blather.
It's a pity, I used to like the sound of words
spoken casually in the street, and whistling.
It took a love of elocution and an ear for music.
It's funny, but devices meant to simplify
have kept us matching wits with living.
But still I'll not give up the gathering of wood
and composing the right size kindling for the fire,
poke the stove with primitive poker, forge a flame.
It's where I'm at. I don't think I need a thermostat.

Whidbey Island
April 2005

THIRD PLACE BOOKS

How quietly you came into my life that day
standing amongst the books in a purple coat.
You turned a page then looked up to say
"That must be you," your coat was open at the throat.
I thought that a clever touch, casual but it meant
some music there, as if you'd sung a note.
We sat for coffee and in the time allowed,
told how our lives had been – we'd done a lot.
You had been to India and I was proud
I'd bummed around the world and all that rot-
casual stuff -I guess we lied a bit about our age,
that little game each knowing that we fabricate.
I made you blush. I inquired too much-
quietly looked you over, guessed your weight
which I didn't need to do – you were petite.
How easily we talked, real down to earth stuff
to get the gist, the score, not sickly sweet.
I knew we shared a style I liked your looks.
I took you to your car – a hug – you left.
I went back and quietly browsed amongst the books.

Lake Forest Park
Washington
25th October 2003

A LADDIE AND A LASSIE

I'll gie ye some words from the Highland Hills
To help ye along your way
You don't need to stash a whole lot of cash
Away for a rainy day.
Be like Robbie Burns, make love in the fields,
Never talk about what ye spent,
The argument wastes the time that is gold,
What ye got is not where it went.
Wha ye have is the precious love you can hold.
It's not the cash ye keep in your kilt.
That skirt is there, it's what ye wear
Hiding jewels, use them weel or they'll wilt.

Wedding of Tracy and Chad
Whidbey Island
August 2006

BONNIE JEAN
(respecting Burns)

Aye it's bonnie ye are
Wi yer dancing feet
An the wee smile ye're hidin.
I'd gae many a mile
Before I'd meet
Wi a lassie quite as charmin.

Let's dance our way
'Neath the hill by the sea
An nae be worried with wha's tae be
Of our different lives, because you see
We don't gie a hoot what the other's aboot
An tha's the best o' guid company.

Scotland
July 2006

FOUR SCORE AND MORE

And so we go into our second life -
another lover, another wife.
Or is she the one we had before
in a different guise - an encore
in our play of life - our striding
this stage, our show, our performing?
Perhaps we felt like Faust for the final act
'till she appeared in the wings - the entr'acte,

There's no curtain, no bows, the act goes on
this loving, this dancing, this laughter, this song.

Whidbey Island
Washington
November 2004